FIXED IDEAS

JOAN DIDION
FIXED IDEAS
AMERICA
SINCE 9.11

PREFACE BY FRANK RICH

as published in The New York Review of Books of January 16, 2003

NEW YORK REVIEW BOOKS, NEW YORK

THIS IS A NEW YORK REVIEW BOOK

PUBLISHED BY THE NEW YORK REVIEW OF BOOKS

FIXED IDEAS: AMERICA SINCE 9.11

by Joan Didion

Copyright © 2003 by Joan Didion
Preface copyright © 2003 by Frank Rich
Copyright © 2003 by NYREV, Inc.

Published in 2003 in the United States of America by
The New York Review of Books, 1755 Broadway, New York, NY 10019
www.nyrb.com

This book is based on the Robert B. Silvers Lecture given
by Joan Didion at the New York Public Library on November 13, 2002.

Book and cover design by Milton Glaser, Inc.

A catalog record for this book is available
from the Library of Congress

ISBN 1-59017-073-3

Printed in the United States of America on acid-free paper.

May 2003

1 3 5 7 9 10 8 6 4 2

PREFACE

AS WE HAVE BEEN INSTRUCTED at regular intervals since September 11, 2001, "they" attacked us because they hate everything we stand for, our freedoms most of all. If that is the case, history will have to explain why post-9/11 America was so quick to rein in the freedom of debate even as we paid constant self-congratulatory lip service to this moral distinction between them and us. September was not over before Ari Fleischer, the President's press secretary, set the tone. "There are reminders to all Americans that they need to watch what they say, watch what they do, and this is not a time for remarks like that," he said, commenting about a wisecrack by a late-night TV comic, Bill Maher, that had gone against the administration's grain. Lest Fleischer's own remarks prompt an unruly debate, history was rewritten for the public record; the official White House Web-site transcript of the briefing deleted Fleischer's warning, an omission the White House later attributed to "a transcription error" (but took days to correct) after some reporters noticed it. It's hard to imagine how those who "hate our freedoms" could have attempted this Orwellian sleight of hand with greater panache.

But in truth, it was not really necessary for Fleischer to issue his warning. The movement to marginalize or mock any quibbles, however slight, with administration wisdom, to minimize unwanted news that might reflect ill on the competence or motives of its leaders, was the nearly spontaneous reaction of the press and television, needing only a little nudge from the White House. It was a sign of the times that for months even the NBC corporate peacock donned the stars and stripes to serve the agreed-upon triumphal mood, should anyone question the old bird's patriotism. When Condoleezza Rice warned that Osama bin Laden might be issuing encoded instructions to his minions through his al-Jazeera video manifestoes, most networks heeded her request to censor them, as if unexpurgated al-Jazeera wasn't widely available to interested parties in the US by satellite anyway. Meanwhile, the administration's law enforcement excesses and failures—the roundup of thousands of immigrants who had nothing to do with al-Qaeda, the inability to discover the source of the anthrax attacks—disappeared into the journalistic memory hole even faster than the White House's bogus assertion that a credible threat against Air Force One had precipitated George W. Bush's disappearing act on September 11.

And so what Joan Didion calls the "fixed ideas" of our war on terrorism were able to fall into place with scant resistance. The reassuring point of the fixed ideas was to suppress other ideas that might prompt questions or fears about either the logic or hidden political agendas of those conducting what CNN branded as "America's New War." Thus the President's "moral clarity," which led the dean of Washington political punditry, David Broder, to liken him to Lincoln, was beyond question: if he declared that "you're either with us or you're with the terrorists," that surely had to be the case, and don't look too closely at our allies Pakistan and Saudi Arabia. The moral bankruptcy of his few vocal critics was also a given. Tom Daschle, the Democratic leader who never seriously challenged administration policy after September 11 and ultimately signed on to the war with Iraq, was likened to Saddam Hussein in TV commercials run in his state. "How dare Senator Daschle criticize President Bush when we are fighting our war on terrorism?" asked Trent Lott, knowing his rhetorical question required no answer by right-thinking Americans.

The President, far from being the "moron" his most moronic adversaries claim, shrewdly capitalized on this atmosphere as the months piled up. This White House is famously secretive and on-message, but its skills go beyond that. It knows the power of narrative, especially a single narrative with clear-cut heroes and evildoers, and it knows how to drown out any distracting subplots before they undermine the main story. Just hours before the FBI agent Colleen Rowley was to testify about her agency's catastrophic sloppiness in the weeks prior to 9/11, the White House abruptly announced its approval of a Department of Homeland Security, a Democratic idea it had previously fought. Rowley and her testimony soon disappeared from prominent view as the networks busily began publicizing the pro forma presidential address hastily assembled for prime-time airing that night.

The Iraq plot, in the works for months, was unveiled with all the care of a Hollywood holiday release. "From a marketing point of view, you don't introduce a new product in August," said Andrew Card, the chief of staff, in late summer 2002, when asked why his boss had prolonged the raising of the curtain. It was an honest answer. Besides, Iraq could not be allowed to distract from the happy story line of that moment, a televised forum in Waco, Texas, at which the President, his soon-to-be-fired economic team, and a gathering of campaign contributors told us to forget our post-Enron worries because relief was on the way. Though in fact no new economic policies were announced, that wasn't the point. It's the *mise en scène* that mattered: White House–produced backdrops emblazoned with legends like "Small Investors / Retirement Security," designed to soothe channel surfers who did not linger to hear the latest variations on the administration's unchanging tax-cut panaceas.

When Iraq was finally rolled out in earnest, it too drowned out some other, conflicting narratives. By mid-January 2003, according to a poll conducted for Knight Ridder by Princeton Survey Research Associates, half the country held the erroneous belief that one or more of the 9/11 hijackers were Iraqi citizens. Bin Laden and Mullah Omar, once prime evildoers, were retired from public discourse almost as completely as the TV series that long ago had prompted the President's desire to apprehend them "dead or alive." So was the lost battle of Tora Bora that hastened their escape. Forgotten too was a new Gary Hart–Warren Rudman task force report on the many weaknesses in domestic security post-9/11—much as their prescient pre-9/11 catalog of similar warnings had been forgotten before the attack. The fragility of post-Taliban Afghanistan and the huge burdens of shouldering a postwar Iraq, let alone the potential perils and costs (of all kinds) of the new war itself, went unmentioned as the President and his war managers repeated over and over that "time is running out."

Time is running out, all right. To suggest that Colin Powell's UN presentation could be an argument for further or perhaps permanent inspections rather than for an imminent invasion is to risk being caught "on the side of the terrorists," or of Hitler's appeasers, or, almost as seditiously, of the French. But North Korea and al-Qaeda, among other players, may not stick to the relatively quiescent roles they have been assigned in the administration's plan for invasion. Wars rarely go according to script. The next stage of this one may determine just how many of our anesthetizing fixed ideas will stay intact and just how cruelly others will be ripped loose from their moorings.

—FRANK RICH

FIXED IDEAS

1

SEVEN DAYS AFTER SEPTEMBER 11, 2001, I left New York to do two weeks of book promotion, under other circumstances a predictable kind of trip. You fly into one city or another, you do half an hour on local NPR, you do a few minutes on drive-time radio, you do an "event," a talk or a reading or an onstage discussion. You sign books, you take questions from the audience. You go back to the hotel, order a club sandwich from room service, and leave a 5 AM call with the desk, so that in the morning you can go back to the airport and fly to the next city. During the week between September 11 and the Wednesday morning when I went to Kennedy to get on the plane, none of these commonplace aspects of publishing a book seemed promising or even appropriate things to be doing. But—like most of us who were in

New York that week—I was in a kind of protective coma, sleepwalking through a schedule made when planning had still seemed possible. In fact I was protecting myself so successfully that I had no idea how raw we all were until that first night, in San Francisco, when I was handed a book onstage and asked to read a few marked lines from an essay about New York I had written in 1967.

Later I remembered thinking: 1967, no problem, no land mines there.

I put on my glasses. I began to read.

"New York was no mere city," the marked lines began. "It was instead an infinitely romantic notion, the mysterious nexus of all love and money and power, the shining and perishable dream itself."

I hit the word "perishable" and I could not say it.

I found myself onstage at the Herbst Theater in San Francisco unable to finish reading the passage, unable to speak at all for what must have been thirty seconds. All

I can say about the rest of that evening, and about the two weeks that followed, is that they turned out to be nothing I had expected, nothing I had ever before experienced, an extraordinarily open kind of traveling dialogue, an encounter with an America apparently immune to conventional wisdom. The book I was making the trip to talk about was *Political Fictions*, a series of pieces I had written for *The New York Review* about the American political process from the 1988 through the 2000 presidential elections. These people to whom I was listening—in San Francisco and Los Angeles and Portland and Seattle—were making connections I had not yet in my numbed condition thought to make: connections between that political process and what had happened on September 11, connections between our political life and the shape our reaction would take and was in fact already taking.

These people recognized that even then, within days

after the planes hit, there was a good deal of opportunistic ground being seized under cover of the clearly urgent need for increased security. These people recognized even then, with flames still visible in lower Manhattan, that the words "bipartisanship" and "national unity" had come to mean acquiescence to the administration's preexisting agenda—for example the imperative for further tax cuts, the necessity for Arctic drilling, the systematic elimination of regulatory and union protections, even the funding for the missile shield—as if we had somehow missed noticing the recent demonstration of how limited, given a few box cutters and the willingness to die, superior technology can be.

These people understood that when Judy Woodruff, on the evening the President first addressed the nation, started talking on CNN about what "a couple of Democratic consultants" had told her about how the President would be needing to position himself,

Washington was still doing business as usual. They understood that when the political analyst William Schneider spoke the same night about how the President had "found his vision thing," about how "this won't be the Bush economy any more, it'll be the Osama bin Laden economy," Washington was still talking about the protection and perpetuation of its own interests.

These people got it.

They didn't like it.

They stood up in public and they talked about it.

Only when I got back to New York did I find that people, if they got it, had stopped talking about it. I came in from Kennedy to find American flags flying all over the Upper East Side, at least as far north as 96th Street, flags that had not been there in the first week after the fact. I say "at least as far north as 96th Street" because a few days later, driving down from Washington Heights past the big projects that would provide at least some of the manpower for the "war on terror" that the President had declared—as if terror were a state and not a technique —I saw very few flags: at most, between 168th Street and 96th Street, perhaps a half-dozen. There were that many flags on my building alone. Three at each of the two entrances. I did not interpret this as an absence of feeling for the country above 96th Street. I interpreted it as an absence of trust in the efficacy of rhetorical gestures.

There was much about this return to New York that I had not expected. I had expected to find the annihilating economy of the event—the way in which it had concentrated the complicated arrangements and misarrangements of the last century into a single irreducible image—being explored, made legible. On the contrary, I found that what had happened was being processed, obscured, systematically leached of history and so of meaning, finally rendered less readable than it had seemed on the morning it happened. As if overnight, the irreconcilable event had been made manageable, reduced to the sentimental, to protective talismans, totems, garlands of garlic, repeated pieties that would come to seem in some ways as destructive as the event itself. We now had "the loved ones," we had "the families," we had "the heroes."

In fact it was in the reflexive repetition of the word "hero" that we began to hear what would become in the year that followed an entrenched preference for ignoring the meaning of the event in favor of an impenetrably flattening celebration of its victims, and a troublingly belligerent idealization of historical ignorance. "Taste" and "sensitivity," it was repeatedly suggested, demanded that we not examine what happened. Images of the intact towers were already being removed from advertising, as if we might conveniently forget they had been there. The Roundabout Theatre had canceled a revival of Stephen Sondheim's *Assassins*, on the grounds that it was "not an appropriate time" to ask audiences "to think critically about various aspects of the American experience." The McCarter Theatre at Princeton had canceled a production of Richard Nelson's *The Vienna Notes*, which involves a terrorist act, saying that "it would be insensitive of us to present the play at this moment in our history."

I found in New York that "the death of irony" had already been declared, repeatedly, and curiously, since irony had been declared dead at the precise moment—given that the gravity of September 11 derived specifically from its designed implosion of historical ironies—when we might have seemed most in need of it. "One good thing could come from this horror: it could spell the end of the age of irony," Roger Rosenblatt wrote within days of the event in *Time*, a thought, or not a thought, destined to be frequently echoed but never explicated. Similarly, I found that "the death of post-modernism" had also been declared. ("It seemed bizarre that events so serious would be linked causally with a rarified form of academic talk," Stanley Fish wrote after receiving a call from a reporter asking if September 11 meant the end of postmodernist relativism. "But in the days that followed, a growing number of commentators played serious variations on the same theme: that the ideas foisted upon us by postmodern intellectuals have weakened the country's resolve.") "Postmodernism" was henceforth to be replaced by "moral clarity," and those who persisted in the decadent insistence that the one did not necessarily cancel out the other would be subjected to what William J. Bennett would call—in *Why We Fight: Moral Clarity and the War on Terrorism*—"a vast relearning," "the reinstatement of a thorough and hon-est study of our history, undistorted by the lens of polit-ical correctness and pseudosophisticated relativism."

■

I found in New York, in other words, that the entire event had been seized—even as the less nimble among us were still trying to assimilate it—to stake new ground in old domestic wars. There was the frequent deployment of the phrase "the Blame America Firsters," or "the Blame America First crowd," the wearying enthusiasm for excoriating anyone who suggested that it could be useful to bring at least a minimal degree of historical reference to bear on the event. There was the adroit introduction of convenient straw men. There was Christopher Hitchens, engaging in a dialogue with Noam Chomsky, giving himself the opportunity to generalize whatever got said into "the liberal-left tendency to 'rationalize' the aggression of September 11." There was Donald Kagan at Yale, dismissing his colleague Paul Kennedy as "a classic case of blaming the victim," because the latter had asked his students to try to imagine what resentments they might harbor if America were small and the world dominated by a unified Arab-Muslim state. There was Andrew Sullivan, warning on his Web site that while the American heartland was ready for war, the "decadent left in its enclaves on the coasts" could well mount "what amounts to a fifth column."

There was the open season on Susan Sontag—on a single page of a single issue of *The Weekly Standard* that October she was accused of "unusual stupidity," of "moral vacuity," and of "sheer tastelessness"—all for three paragraphs in which she said, in closing, that "a few shreds of historical awareness might help us understand what has just happened, and what may continue to happen"; in other words that events have histories, political life has consequences, and the people who led this country and the people who wrote and spoke about the way this country was led were guilty of trying to infantilize its citizens if they continued to pretend otherwise.

Inquiry into the nature of the enemy we faced, in other words, was to be interpreted as sympathy for that enemy. The final allowable word on those who attacked us was to be that they were "evildoers," or "wrongdoers," peculiar constructions which served to suggest that those who used them were transmitting messages from some ultimate authority. This was a year in which it would come to seem as if we had been plunged at one fell stroke into a pre-modern world. The possibilities of the Enlightenment vanished. We had suddenly been asked to accept—and were in fact accepting—a kind of reasoning so extremely fragile that it might have been based on the promised return of the cargo gods.

I recall, early on, after John Ashcroft and Condoleezza Rice warned the networks not to air the bin Laden tapes because he could be "passing information," heated debate

about the First Amendment implications of this warning—as if there were even any possible point to the
warning, as if we had all forgotten that our enemies as
well as we lived in a world where information gets
passed in more efficient ways. A year later, we were still
looking for omens, portents, the supernatural manifes-
tations of good or evil. Pathetic fallacy was everywhere.
The presence of rain at a memorial for fallen firefight-
ers was gravely reported as evidence that "even the sky
cried." The presence of wind during a memorial at the
site was interpreted as another such sign, the spirit of
the dead rising up from the dust.

This was a year when Rear Admiral John Stufflebeem,
deputy director of operations for the Joint Chiefs of
Staff, would say at a Pentagon briefing that he had been
"a bit surprised" by the disinclination of the Taliban to
accept the "inevitability" of their own defeat. It seemed

that Admiral Stufflebeem, along with many other people in Washington, had expected the Taliban to just give
up. "The more that I look into it," he said at this briefing, "and study it from the Taliban perspective, they
don't see the world the same way we do." It was a year
when the publisher of *The Sacramento Bee*, speaking at the
midyear commencement of California State University,
Sacramento, would be forced off the stage of the Arco
Arena for suggesting that because of the "validity" and
"need" for increased security we would be called upon
to examine to what degree we might be "willing to
compromise our civil liberties in the name of security."
Here was the local verdict on this aborted speech, as
expressed in one of many outraged letters to the editor
of the *Bee*:

> It was totally and completely inappropriate for her
> to use this opportunity to speak about civil liberties,

military tribunals, terrorist attacks, etc. She should have prepared a speech about the accomplishments that so many of us had just completed, and the future opportunities that await us.

In case you think that's a Sacramento story, it's not.

Because this was also a year when one of the student speakers at the 2002 Harvard commencement, Zayed Yasin, a twenty-two-year-old Muslim raised in a Boston suburb by his Bangladeshi father and Irish-American mother, would be caught in a swarm of protests provoked by the announced title of his talk, which was "My American Jihad." In fact the speech itself, which he had not yet delivered, fell safely within the commencement-address convention: its intention, Mr. Yasin told *The New York Times*, was to reclaim the original meaning of "jihad" as struggle on behalf of a principle, and to use it to rally his classmates in the fight against social injustice.

Such use of "jihad" was not in this country previously uncharted territory: the Democratic pollster Daniel Yankelovich had only a few months before attempted to define the core values that animated what he called "the American jihad"—separation of church and state, the value placed on diversity, and equality of opportunity. In view of the protests, however, Mr. Yasin was encouraged by Harvard faculty members to change his title. He did change it. He called his talk "Of Faith and Citizenship." This mollified some, but not all. "I don't think it belonged here today," one Harvard parent told *The Washington Post*. "Why bring it up when today should be a day of joy?"

This would in fact be a year when it was to become increasingly harder to know who was infantilizing who.

2

CALIFORNIA MONTHLY, the alumni magazine for the
University of California at Berkeley, published in its
November 2002 issue an interview with a member of
the university's political science faculty, Steven Weber,
who is the director of the MacArthur Program on
Multilateral Governance at Berkeley's Institute of
International Studies and a consultant on risk analysis
to both the State Department and such private-sector
firms as Shell Oil. It so happened that Mr. Weber was in
New York on September 11, 2001, and for the week that
followed. "I spent a lot of time talking to people, watching what they were doing, and listening to what they
were saying to each other," he told the interviewer:

The first thing you noticed was in the bookstores.

On September 12, the shelves were emptied of books on Islam, on American foreign policy, on Iraq, on Afghanistan. There was a substantive discussion about what it is about the nature of the American presence in the world that created a situation in which movements like al-Qaeda can thrive and prosper. I thought that was a very promising sign.

But that discussion got short-circuited. Sometime in late October, early November 2001, the tone of that discussion switched, and it became: What's wrong with the Islamic world that it failed to produce democracy, science, education, its own enlightenment, and created societies that breed terror?

The interviewer asked him what he thought had changed the discussion. "I don't know," he said, "but I will say that it's a long-term failure of the political leadership, the intelligentsia, and the media in this country that we didn't take the discussion that was forming in late September and try to move it forward in a constructive way."

I was struck by this, since it so coincided with my own impression. Most of us saw that discussion short-circuited, and most of us have some sense of how and why it became a discussion with nowhere to go. One reason, among others, runs back sixty years, through every administration since Franklin Roosevelt's. Roosevelt was the first American president who tried to grapple with the problems inherent in securing Palestine as a Jewish state. It was also Roosevelt who laid the groundwork for our relationship with the Saudis. There was an inherent contradiction here, and it was Roosevelt, perhaps the most adroit political animal ever made, who instinctively devised the approach adopted by the administrations that followed his: Stall. Keep the options open. Make certain promises in public, and conflicting ones in private. This was always a high-risk business, and for a while the rewards seemed commensurate: we got the oil for helping the Saudis, we got the moral credit for helping the Israelis, and, for helping both, we enjoyed the continuing business that accrued to an American defense industry significantly based on arming all sides.

Consider the range of possibilities for contradiction.

Sixty years of making promises we had no way of keeping without breaking the promises we'd already made.

Sixty years of long-term conflicting commitments, made in secret and in many cases for short-term political reasons.

Sixty years that tend to demystify the question of why we have become unable to discuss our relationship with the current government of Israel.

Whether the actions taken by that government constitute self-defense or a particularly inclusive form of self-immolation remains an open question. The question of course has a history, a background involving many complicit state and non-state actors and going back most recently to, but by no means beginning with, the breakup of the Ottoman Empire. This open question, and its history, are discussed rationally and with considerable intellectual subtlety in Jerusalem and Tel Aviv, as anyone who reads Amos Elon or Avishai Margalit in *The New York Review* or even occasionally sees *Ha'aretz* on-line is well aware. Where the question is not discussed rationally—where in fact the question is rarely discussed at all, since so few of us are willing to see our evenings turn toxic—is in New York and Washington and in those academic venues where the attitudes and apprehensions of New York and Washington have taken hold. The president of Harvard recently warned that criticisms of the current government of Israel could be construed as "anti-Semitic in their effect if not their intent."

The very question of the US relationship with Israel, in other words, has come to be seen—at Harvard as well as in New York and Washington—as unraisable, potentially lethal, the conversational equivalent of an unclaimed bag on a bus. We take cover. We wait for the entire subject to be defused, safely insulated behind baffles of invective and counterinvective. Many opinions are expressed. Few are allowed to develop. Even fewer change.

We have come in this country to tolerate many such fixed opinions, or national pieties, each with its own baffles of invective and counterinvective, of euphemism and downright misstatement, its own screen that slides into place whenever actual discussion threatens to surface. We have for example allowed American biological research to fall behind that in countries where stem cell programs are not confused with "cloning" and "abortion on demand," countries in other words where rationality is not held hostage to the posturing of the political process. We have allowed all rhetorical stops to be pulled out on non-issues, for example when the federal appeals court's Ninth Circuit ruled the words "under God" an unconstitutional addition to the Pledge of Allegiance. The Pledge was written in 1892 by a cousin of Edward Bellamy's, Francis Bellamy, a socialist Baptist minister who the year before had been pressured to give up his church because of the socialist thrust of his sermons. The clause "under God" was added in 1954 to distinguish the United States from the atheistic Soviet Union.

"Ridiculous" was the word from the White House about the ruling declaring the clause unconstitutional. "Junk justice," Governor Pataki said. "Just nuts," Senator Daschle said. "Doesn't make good sense to me," Representative Gephardt said. There was on this point a genuinely bipartisan rush to act out the extent of the judicial insult, the affront to all Americans, the outrage to the memory of the heroes of September 11. After the June 2002 ruling, members of the House met on the Capitol steps to recite the Pledge—needless to say the "under God" version—while the Senate interrupted debate on a defense bill to pass, unanimously, a resolution condemning the Ninth Circuit decision.

These were, some of them, the same elected representatives who had been quick to locate certain upside aspects to September 11. The events could offer, it was almost immediately perceived, an entirely new frame in which to present school prayer and the constitutional amendment to ban flag burning. To the latter point, an Iowa congressman running unsuccessfully for the Senate, Greg Ganske, marked Flag Day by posting a reminder on his Web site that his opponent, Senator Tom Harkin, who had spent five years during the Vietnam War as a

Navy pilot, had in 1995 opposed the flag-burning amendment. "After the tragic events of September 11," the posting read, "America has a renewed sense of patriotism and a renewed appreciation for our American flag. Unfortunately, not everyone agrees." To the school prayer point, according to *The New York Times*, a number of politicians were maximizing the moment by challenging restrictions on school prayer established by courts over the past four decades. "Post–September 11," the *Times* was told by Richard D. Land, president of the Ethics and Religious Liberty Commission of the Southern Baptist Convention, "the secularists are going to have a harder time making their case."

One footnote on the Pledge issue, and the extent to which it intersects with the case the secularists are going to have a harder time making: a significant number of Americans now recite the Pledge with another new clause, which they hope to see made permanent by legislation. After the words "with liberty and justice for all," they add "born and unborn."

All of these issues or non-issues are, as they say, just politics, markers in a game. The flag-burning amendment is just politics, the school prayer issue is just politics—a bone to the Republican base on the Christian right and a way to beat up on the judiciary, red meat for the "Reagan Democrats" or "swing voters" who are increasingly seen as the base for both parties. The prohibition on the creation of new cell lines from discarded embryos that constituted the President's "compromise" on the stem cell question is politics. The fact that Israel has become the fulcrum of our foreign policy is politics. When it comes to any one of these phenomena that we dismiss as "politics," we tend to forgive, or at least overlook, the absence of logic or sense. We tell ourselves that this is the essential give and take of democracy, we tell ourselves that our elected representatives are doing the necessary work of creating consensus. We try to convince ourselves that somewhere, beneath the posturing, there is a hidden logic, there are minds at work, there is someone actually thinking out the future of the country beyond the 2004 election.

These would be comforting notions were they easier to maintain. In fact we have created a political process in which "consensus" is the last thing the professionals want or need, a process that works precisely by turning the angers and fears and energy of the few—that handful of voters who can be driven by the fixed aspect of their own opinions—against the rest of the country. During the past decade—through the several years of the impeachment process and through the denouement of the 2000 election—we had seen secular democracy itself put up for grabs in this country, and the response to September 11 could not have encouraged us to think that the matter was in any way settled.

We had seen the general acquiescence in whatever was presented as imperative by the administration. We had seen the persistent suggestions that anyone who expressed reservations about detentions, say, or military tribunals, was at some level "against" America. (As in the presidential formulation "you're either with us or you're with the terrorists.") We had seen, most importantly, the insistent use of September 11 to justify the reconception of America's correct role in the world as one of initiating and waging virtually perpetual war. And we had seen, buttressing this reconception, the demand that we interpret the war in Afghanistan as a decisive victory over al-Qaeda, the Taliban, and radical fundamentalism in general.

This was despite repeated al-Qaeda-linked explosions throughout Southeast Asia.

Despite continuing arson and rocket attacks on girls' schools in Afghanistan.

And despite the fact that the chairman of the Joint Chiefs said in November 2002 at the Brookings Institution that we had lost momentum in Afghanistan because the Taliban and al-Qaeda had been quicker to adapt to US tactics than the US had been to theirs.

3

IN 1988, A FEW WEEKS AFTER GEORGE W. BUSH'S FATHER was
elected president, I wrote a post-election note for *The
New York Review* about a trip the senior Bush had made
to Israel and Jordan in 1986, when he was still vice-
president. He had his own camera crew with him in
Israel, but not in Jordan, since, as an official explained
to the *Los Angeles Times*, there was "nothing to be gained
from showing him schmoozing with Arabs." Still, the
Bush advance team in Amman had devoted considerable
attention to crafting visuals for the traveling press.
Members of the advance team had requested, for example, that the Jordanian army marching band change its
uniforms from white to red. They had requested that
the Jordanians, who did not have enough helicopters
to transport Bush's traveling press corps, borrow the

necessary helicopters to do so from the Israeli air force. In an effort to assure the color of live military action as a backdrop for the vice-president, they had asked the Jordanians to stage maneuvers at a sensitive location overlooking Israel and the Golan Heights. They had asked the Jordanians to raise, over the Jordanian base there, the American flag. They had asked that Bush be photographed studying, through binoculars, "enemy territory," a shot ultimately vetoed by the State Department, since the "enemy territory" at hand was Israel. They had also asked, possibly the most arresting detail, that, at every stop on the itinerary, camels be present.

"This is in fact the kind of story we expect to hear about our elected officials," I wrote in 1988:

> We not only expect them to use other nations as changeable scrims in the theater of domestic politics but encourage them to do so. After the April

1961 failure of the Bay of Pigs, John Kennedy's approval rating was four points higher than it had been in March. After the 1965 intervention in the Dominican Republic, Lyndon Johnson's approval rating rose six points. After the 1983 invasion of Grenada, Ronald Reagan's approval rating rose four points, and what was that winter referred to in Washington as "Lebanon"—the sending of American marines into Beirut, the killing of 241, and the subsequent pullout—was, in the afterglow of this certified success in the Caribbean, largely forgotten.

That was 1988. Fourteen years later, we were again watching the scrims being changed, but in a theater we did not own. The Middle East was not Grenada. It was not the Dominican Republic. It was not, as they used to say in Washington about the Caribbean, "our lake." It was nitroglycerin, an unstable part of the world in which we had managed to make few friends and many enemies. And yet, all through the summer of 2002, the inevitability of going to war with Iraq was accepted as if predestined. The "when" had already been settled. "Time is getting short," *The New York Times* had warned us in July, "for decisions that have to be made if the goal is to take action early next year, before the presidential election cycle intrudes." That last clause bore study.

"Before the presidential election cycle intrudes." In case the priorities were still unclear.

The "why" had also been settled. The President had identified Saddam Hussein as one of the evildoers. Yes, there were questions about whether the evildoer in question had the weapons we feared he had, and yes, there were questions about whether he would use them if he did have them, and yes, there were questions about whether attacking Iraq might not in fact ensure that he would use them. But to ask those questions was sissy, not muscular, because the President had said we were going to do it and the President, if he were to back down, risked losing the points he got on the muscular "moral clarity" front.

"I made up my mind," he had said in April, "that Saddam needs to go." This was one of many curious, almost petulant statements offered in lieu of actually presenting a case. I've made up my mind, I've said in speech after speech, I've made myself clear. The repeated statements became their own reason: "Given all we have said as a leading world power about the necessity for regime change in Iraq," James R. Schlesinger, who is now a member of Richard Perle's Defense Policy Board, told *The Washington Post* in July, "our credibility would be badly damaged if that regime change did not take place."

There was of course, for better or for worse, a theory,

or a fixed idea, behind these pronouncements from the President—actually not so much behind them as coinciding with them, dovetailing in a way that made it possible for many to suggest that the President was actually in on the thinking. The theory, or fixed idea, which not only predated September 11 but went back to the Reagan administration and its heady dreams of rollback, had already been employed to provide a rationale for the President's tendency to exhibit a certain truculence toward those who were not Americans. Within the theory, any such truculence could be inflated into "The Bush Doctrine," or "The New American Unilateralism." The theory was this: the collapse of the Soviet Union had opened the door to the inevitability of American preeminence, a mantle of beneficent power that all nations except rogue nations—whatever they might say on the subject— were yearning for us to assume. "We run a uniquely benign imperium," Charles Krauthammer had written in celebration of this point in a June 2001 issue of *The Weekly Standard*. "This is not mere self-congratulation; it is a fact manifest in the way others welcome our power."

Given this fixed idea, as if in a dream from which there is no waking, and given the correlative dream notion that an American president, Ronald Reagan, had himself caused the collapse of the Soviet Union with a specific magical incantation, the "Evil Empire" speech, the need to bring our force for good to bear on the Middle East could only become an imperative. By June 2002, Jim Hoagland was noting in *The Washington Post* that there was a growing acceptance at the White House of the need for an overwhelming US invasion force that will remain on the ground in Iraq for several years. The US presence will serve as the linchpin for democratic transformation of a major Arab country that can be a model for the region. A new Iraq would also help provide greater energy security for Americans.

A few weeks later in the *Post*, Michael Kelly was sketching an even rosier outcome, based on his eccentric reading of the generation now coming of age in the Middle East as a population poised by history to see the United States not as its enemy but as its "natural liberator." "It is right to think that we are living in a hinge moment in history," he wrote, and then argued against those who believe that the moment is not necessarily ours to control. "But it is wrong to think that the large forces of this moment act on the hinge to shut the door against American interests." The contrary may be true, he wrote, if only we take the next step, which is "to destroy the regime of Saddam Hussein and liberate the people of Iraq." This will be, he said, "when history really begins to turn on its hinge."

It so happened that I was traveling around the country again recently, talking and listening to people in St.

Louis and Columbia and Philadelphia and San Diego and Los Angeles and San Francisco and Pittsburgh and Boston. I heard very few of the fixed ideas about America's correct role in the world that had come to dominate the dialogue in New York and Washington. I encountered many people who believed there was still what we had come to call a disconnect between the government and the citizens. I did not encounter conviction that going to war with Iraq would result in a democratic transformation of the Middle East. Most people seemed resigned to the prospect that we would nonetheless go to war with Iraq. Many mentioned a sense of "inevitability," or "dread." A few mentioned August 1914, and its similar sense of an irreversible drift toward something that would not work out well. Several mentioned Vietnam, and the similar bright hopefulness of those who had seen yet another part of the world as a blackboard on which to demonstrate their own superior plays. A few said that had they lost relatives on September 11, which they had not, they would be deeply angered at having those deaths cheapened by being put to use to justify this new war. They did not understand what this new war was about, but they knew it wasn't about that promising but never quite substantiated meeting in Prague between Iraqi intelligence and Mohamed Atta. They did not want to believe that it was about oil. Nor did they want to believe that it was about domestic politics. If I had to characterize a common attitude among them I would call it waiting to see. At a remove.

Like most of them, I no longer remembered all the arguments and inconsistencies and downright contradictions of the summer and early fall. I did remember one thing: a sequence of reports. It was June 1 when the President announced, in a commencement address at West Point, that the United States military would henceforth act not defensively but preemptively against terrorists and hostile states in possession of chemical, biological, or nuclear weapons. It was June 6 when the secretary of state advised NATO in Brussels that NATO could no longer wait for "absolute proof" of such possession before taking action. It was June 10 when Thomas E. Ricks and Vernon Loeb reported in The Washington Post that under this new doctrine, according to Pentagon officials, the United States would consider using high-yield nuclear weapons on a first-strike basis. The use of such weapons would be reserved, according to these officials, for deployment "against biological weapons that can be best destroyed by sustained exposure to the high heat of a nuclear blast." Some bunkers in Iraq, the Post was told by Stephen M. Younger, the director of the Defense Department's Defense Threat Reduction Agency, are in fact "so incredibly hard" that "they do require high-yield nuclear weapons."

I never saw this mentioned again. I never heard anyone refer to it. Not even during the discussions of nuclear intentions that occurred six months later, after the administration released a reminder that the US reserved the right, if it or its allies were attacked with weapons of mass destruction, to respond with nuclear as well as conventional force. But let's look at where we are.

The idealists of the process are talking about the hinge of history.

And the Department of Defense was talking as early as last June about unloosing, for the first time since 1945, high-yield nuclear weapons.

In the early 1980s I happened to attend, at a Conservative Political Action conference in Washington, a session called "Rolling Back the Soviet Empire." One of the speakers that day was a kind of adventurer-slash-ideologue named Jack Wheeler, who was very much of the moment because he had always just come back from

spending time with our freedom fighters in Afghanistan, also known as the Mujahideen. I recall that he
received a standing ovation after urging that copies of
the Koran be smuggled into the Soviet Union to "stim-
ulate an Islamic revival" and the subsequent "death of a
thousand cuts." We all saw that idea come home.